Fin

C000133634

Pa~~ssion~~

Discover Purpose & Live the Life
of Your Wildest Dreams

Chandler Kitching

Dedication

To my parents, for always cultivating my curiosity.
I love you both dearly and can't wait to show you
the world.

Table of Contents

Banish Perfectionism & Shame

Show Imposter Syndrome Who's Boss

Be Polarizing

Sustain the Momentum

Summary

Action Steps

My Ultimate Focus Tool Kit

(Never waste another day without this.)

As a way of saying thanks for reading my journey to finding passion, I would like to offer you my complete ultimate focus checklist for free.

My checklist includes:

1. 11 elegant tools to unlock your personal master focus plan.
2. My personal external brain arsenal for maximum efficiency.
3. My favorite subliminal & isochronic tone sources for deep concentration.

This is the list I wish I had at the beginning of my

journey to true attention.

To receive your help tool kit, visit the link or scan the QR code below.

https://chandlerkitching.activehosted.com/f/1

Foreword

Life is strange. We are all asked as children, "what are you going to be when you grow up?"

Our answers were mostly firefighter, police officer, pirate, dancer, actor, musician, teacher, mad scientist, princess, professional athlete, detective, astronaut, pilot, veterinarian, or even a favorite superhero.

When children are asked what they want to be when they grow up, they usually respond to the question with, "I *am going* to be..." If you don't believe me, ask a 4-year-old what they are going to be.

Children are wonderful because they are so sure of themselves much of the time. Somewhere along the line, when we get slightly older, we respond with, "I want to be...". Hold on one minute, we went from "I am *going* to be a princess" to "I *want* to be a veterinarian"? We are so sure of ourselves in our fairy tale fantasies. Anything is possible until external forces influence our realities. This is a shocking discovery. A discovery that displays how early doubt grows in the subconscious mind. "I want to" is a gateway drug to saying "I don't know".

Somewhere along the line we are told that life is a very serious ordeal, and we need to be realistic.

We are usually told that our dreams are not workable and some authority figures will even plant doubt into our minds as young susceptible sponges. There is no malevolent intent. When 4-year-olds say they want to be a mad scientist, most people will tell them to choose an actual profession. Killing an individual's dream has the power to kill their soul and set forth a life of "what ifs" and unfulfillment. When children are that young, we must instill a belief system around anything being possible. When the child grows up, they will learn on their own that they can't be princess Diana. The key is to cultivate their curiosity, imagination, and a firm belief that they can do anything they put their mind to. Many people try to protect their child from disappointment. My argument? Settling for a mediocre life, while the "what if" monster eats away at their soul is far worse.

Once the fairy tale dreams are thoroughly squashed out of our soul, the next primary focus is to find the most secure job possible that also pays the most money. You are investing your time and money! You better make the right decision... or else. If you are interested in this career, they urge you to put your fairy tale interests on the back burner because our perceived authorities "only want the best for us".

To be clear, I was one of the lucky few that was told I can do anything or be anyone, no matter how ridiculous my suggestions were. Yes, I wanted to be a pirate. I am tremendously grateful for this. Not just grateful that I decided to not be a pirate, but more grateful for my parents homeschooling me and cultivating my inner dreamer. I used to wear a different costume every day of the week.

One day I was a clown, next day an astronaut, or cowboy. You get the picture. Every day, I woke up, looked into the mirror and asked myself who I wanted to be. There were plenty of not so helpful opinions from future teachers and extended family. I am sure that you can relate to the latter.

Once I hit about 15, all my extended family began asking me, "What do you want to go to college for?" This question often has a sinister presumption that we will do this activity for the rest of our lives.

I used to dread this question during the extended family get-togethers because I often got unsolicited opinions. My parents never cared about the opinions of others, but I am sure many people feel like they need to impress their parent's friends and family. This is a recipe for a lifestyle disaster down the road.

Over my teenage years, I got so annoyed with these never-ending assumptions and questions about my career that I started saying ridiculous answers. In my mind as a 15-year-old, that was a ridiculous question, so I gave them a ridiculous answer.

My favorites were, "I am going to study imperialism and become an emperor," "I am going to become a guru, sit on a bed of nails on top of a mountain," or "I am going to start a rogue religious cult and have my disciples build a landing pad for a spaceship."

Many people would open their eyes real wide and slowly nod in either pure fear or disbelief. This usually deterred them from asking again. I mean, who really can say that they would like the same profession for 40 years? Many people can never decide on what tattoo to get because they know it's forever. When you are cautious about tattoos, society applauds you. However, when you can't decide on a profession that will last a lifetime, there is this underground "loser" stigma. There are many people who have found a profession they love for their entire lives, so we know that this is possible. How many people do you know feel this way?

After asking me these questions, many relatives would give me advice, some good and some bad. The worst advice that I received was when someone told me to "never change majors in college, stick with whatever you chose." I agree that when bright, bushy eyed children go to college, they should know what they want to be and understand that they need a degree to get that job. However, sticking with a career that we have chosen in the past just because of a sunk cost fallacy can be the worst mistake of our lives. The mindset is I have already spent so many years at this job, or I spent so much on getting my degree that I can't switch now. I agree, when debt comes into the equation, then it becomes further more complicated.

We only have one life as far as we know. Time is precious and we can't waste another minute being someone we don't want to be or being in a career we hate. If we are making good money at a current job and want to hit a financial goal before we switch, then that is understandable. The key is to have an escape plan and stick to it. I am here to show you your alternative plan.

My best friend and roommate in college made a brave and terrifying decision.

After graduating with a 4.0, 4 years of intense 18 credit course loads while working part time, and 80,000 dollars spent at a university, he pulled the plug on his chosen career. You may think my friend is insane and with only a shallow perspective, I can totally understand your position. 80k is a massive amount of money, but you know what 80k can't buy? 1 minute of time. Time is our most valuable resource by far, and it's dwindling fast. My roommate couldn't bear the thought of spending another week of his life working 16-hour days, with obscure hours of nights and days alternating and sometimes back to back. His love for his major, that he enjoyed doing in his free time ever since he was 13, was absolutely crushed when he realized the realities of prospective jobs. He made all the right moves and achieved all the right things; however, nothing was going to prepare him for the reality of his chosen career except actually DOING it. At first, I didn't understand, but later realized that I respect him deeply for his decision. Sometimes the dreams in our head don't line up with the realities of life.

At my last job, there was a wall filled with pictures of employees that had been with the company for 25 years or more. When examining these pictures closely you could see the dissatisfaction on most faces. Some had a "deer in the headlights" look, while others looked angry or even resentful. When I interviewed these people, their story was almost always the same. They had a dream when they were younger. They got this job as a young person to get them good pay and significant benefits for the time being. They put their actual goals on the back burner because they needed money now. Then they met a partner, fell in love, and had children. Now they feel like they have to keep working at the same career that was originally viewed as temporary. Going back to school, picking up a trade, or switching to a new career is viewed as risky. They spend all their days talking about how much they resent their employer and how they wished that they kept pursuing their dream in their youth. Days turn to months, months turn to years, and years turn into a quarter century, then they get to have their picture taken and put on the wall.

This story is not always the case, and I realize that the culture of my last job is most likely different from yours. Personally, I can definitely resonate with their story because I feel like this is the untold story of millions of people. If you are born into a first world country or into a family with more money there is incredible opportunity to have. In my experience of talking to my coworkers, this head start does not guarantee happiness or guarantee finding a career that they love.

Dissatisfaction turns into a never-ending downward spiral. When we despise what we do every day, we will look for anything to distract us from our reality. For most people, that usually means slamming energy drinks during the week to stay alert, and drinking alcohol after work while watching tv. Fast food, internet porn, or video games you name it when you meet people who are dissatisfied usually, they occupy all their free time with escapes from reality. There is inherently nothing wrong with most of these activities. When it becomes an escape from being the hero in your own life, then escaping becomes a drug. It feels more delightful and comforting than being cradled in your mother's womb. The major hidden problem lies in trying to live vicariously through others while never living our own life to the fullest.

I have been through this wormhole, and I am here to tell you it is possible to escape the life of sheer daily dissatisfaction. It doesn't matter if you skipped college, dropped out, or graduated. It doesn't matter if you are having a quarter life crisis, a midlife crisis, or want to make some money in retirement. It doesn't matter if you have kids or don't have kids, what I am going to teach you in this book has the power to change your life forever.

I recreated the system that I used to find my life of passion originally for my friends and family. They would often ask me how I found my passion and if I had any advice on how to find their passion. I wanted to write a quick guide that I could send them instead of telling them in person. I wanted to give them a roadmap that they could refer back to if they fell off course. My original thought was to make this a long blog post, but I just couldn't boil the information down anymore than I already have. Once I started getting feedback, I realized that this had potential to help on people on an exponential level instead of linear.

You are going to learn how to face your problem head on, to have the courage to ask yourself the right questions and to be alone with your thoughts. I have created a system that will give you the life of your wildest dreams if you take consistent action. I am going to teach you how to discover your passion by defining who you are, what you are good at, your ideal environment, your interests, your life values, your favorite problem to solve, and finally how to make the decision.

It doesn't matter if you are where you want to be in life. It is possible to feel more passion for your life while you aggressively pursue the life of your wildest dreams.

I know how you feel. I've felt your struggles and your desires because I have been in your shoes. I have lived the unfulfilled life, a life of dread for the day ahead. Anger at myself and those around me, riding a constant high of stress induced adrenaline and espresso shots. When life slowed down, feelings of deep apathy reared their ugly head. I interviewed countless others from all walks of life who feel the same as I did.

There are people that rise above their challenges and escape the hamster wheel of their current career. Some try briefly, but most never try at all, in my experience. The fact that you are reading this book means that you are among those who are meant to be happy. You chose to take the first step by identifying your problem and charging the gates of uncertainty.

Personally, I dropped out of college with $33,000 in student loans. I earned a decent scholarship through my academic achievements, but that still wasn't enough to satisfy the hunger of the institution.

I lived in a rundown, bed bugged, and black-mold-infested apartment, worked for minimum wage, took public transit and had no money to my name except for plain brown rice and a roof over my head. I am honestly so happy that I went through this because I wouldn't have had nearly as much drive to change my situation. I understand what it's like!

I took a career that put me on track to make a healthy living for myself. Desperate at the time, this opportunity felt like my only hope for digging myself out of the hole I created. This wonderful opportunity slowly turned into a soul harvesting state of affairs. I used to feel so hopeless that I would calculate how many decades it would take me hating every minute of my career to retire and do what I love. If I was extremely frugal and missed out on living my life, I calculated that I would retire by 50, instead of 65. I was burned out and terrified that I wouldn't escape. I felt destined to a life longing for Friday while a deep piercing pit in my stomach would hit me every time the alarm clock went off at 3 am.

I went to work every day with this goal of 50 in my head for almost 5 years until one day I decided to unplug the cord harvesting my energy and wake the hell up!

I escaped the matrix of self-doubt, dissatisfaction, unfulfillment, and hopelessness by taking constant deliberate action towards finding my passion. I worked on my passion deep into the night, early into the morning and ultimately freed myself.

I now live a life of joy and passion every day, and I am excited to wake up in the morning. I love everything about my life, but the journey was not comfortable. I used to hate every minute of my life, and now I love it. I realize that many of you are in worse situations than I was in. I understand that I am still incredibly blessed to have been born in a first world country.

Imagine a life where you wake up thrilled to take on the day, and you don't set an alarm because living your life is better than the dream world. You will choose to either work longer hours at your career to smash through your goals or spend more time doing things you love. Such as being with your family and friends or pursuing a new crazy hobby.

Your life flows together seamlessly and your productivity skyrockets simultaneously. You feel grateful to have your life and wouldn't trade it for anything in the world. When Sunday night hits, you will have feelings of excitement wash over you in lieu of dread. You can't wait to get back to work because you cherish the time you get to work. Your career is something you GET to do, not you HAVE to do.

Your goals will become bigger than monetary values because you feel you are contributing to something greater than yourself. I never set financial goals anymore. I set all my goals based on the amount of people I want to make a positive impact on. This life is not mystical, it is a realistic option that you can choose to pursue, discover and seize for yourself.

I know that when you follow my system, you will feel you have a fresh new life. I am living proof. You never have to settle for a mediocre life filled with denying desires. If you follow the find your passion road map, you will look back a year from now and not even recognize yourself anymore.

You must understand that time is of the essence. Every minute you spend upset and unfulfilled is a minute that you will never get back. We are all born with the same terminal condition and that is called time. Now that you have the answers in your hand, nothing is stopping you from obtaining your new life of joy. If you stop reading this book and stop pursuing your life of passion, then nothing I can do will help you.

Every day, you will make a choice. You can stop chasing your dreams, hit snooze and take the blue pill or you can take the red pill of choosing daily consistent effort. The choice is yours. Will you keep slamming snooze and dreaming of your life, or will you rise and live your dream? Once I had a small taste of my dream life, then every day I didn't take action felt like a splinter growing in my mind, driving me mad as time whizzed by.

Step 1: Slaying the Common Passion Myths

Demystifying Passion & the Disease of Not Knowing

People infect themselves with the disease of "not knowing" what they love. That is understandable, because pretty much nobody is born knowing their passion is. You may think Bill Gates was born with the passion of inventing Windows, but what if he was born 1,000 years ago? What if he was born in a third world country in the slums? This realization is terrifying to many people because there are endless possibilities. Many people have this romantic vision of what their life of passion truly looks like. They think it should feel like the first 3 months of dating your partner. When the honeymoon phase fades away, sometimes we feel hollow, like this isn't our genuine passion.

There are highs and lows to every endeavor and passion. The key question is, do the highs carry and commit you deeper during the lows? Passion isn't a life plan that will dawn on you while you rest on a bed of nails in a deep Himalayan cave.

What you are looking for is not a person, place or thing, at least a long-term passion.

The problem is that passion is mistaken for an emotion, and emotions come and go with the wind.

Passion is not something that will be the same over your entire life for many.

It feels daunting for many people because they feel like they have a limited amount of time to make a decision. A decision that will haunt them for the rest of their lives.

Passion is an action that gives you energy. Notice the things you do in your daily life. What gives you energy and what takes energy from you? Follow the feeling of freedom. Follow what makes you feel complete, even if you get moments of stress from doing the challenging and worthwhile. The more challenging the pursuit, the juicier the reward.

Every task of your passion won't give you energy, but does your passion give or take energy from you overall? When you hit a high from a passion, you won't want to stop working on it. You will obsess over it before, during, and after normal work hours. You feel invigorated when your alarm clock goes off. In fact, you don't need an alarm clock, the obsession of your dream wakes you up. That initial spark at the beginning of the journey will become your "why" and from there you cultivate your passion to blossom into a majestic garden of skill, joy and purpose.

Your dream career is a vessel for your expression. It is your gift to the world. What do you want your legacy to look like?

Common Dream Killing Beliefs

Before we can propel ourselves into a whole new life of passion, we must undo all the false beliefs around who you are and what you are doing with your life.

The most common false belief around passion that if you don't know what your passion is by a certain age, then something is wrong with you. A study at Stanford concluded that on average, "Less than 20% of [people] actually know their passion and how to fulfill it." 80% of people have many interests and no idea what their passion is.

The next false belief pertains to college students, but applies to everyone.

"The degree you are pursuing has to be what you are going to do for the rest of your life."

There couldn't be worse advice. Jaison Abel and Richard Dietz of the Federal Reserve Bank of New York analyzed the data from the U.S. Bureau of the 2010 Census. They found that on average only 27% of college graduates have a career related to their major.

They often translate the same belief to everyone else as, "whatever job you choose when you are fresh out of college or high school will be the career path that you follow forever."

This could not be further from the truth. According to career change statistics, "The average person will change careers 5-7 times during their working life." There is a great nobility in knowing when to make that career change and pursuing it relentlessly. It takes courage, drive, and brutal honesty.

Because of all these false beliefs, many people feel shame that they are not where they want to be in life. There is no reason to feel shame on your journey. The fact that you picked up this book and began reading means you are well ahead of the pack. Passion is a marathon, not a 100-meter dash. Shame will only impede your progress and suck your energy further. You are going to need all the energy you can muster up for the trials ahead. I believe in you and will be here for you every step of the way.

The Passion vs. Success Debate

There is a long, ongoing debate with many researchers and professionals. If we find valuable, meaningful work then the passion will follow. They believe that you don't follow your passion, your passion follows you.

The other side of the debate says that to get genuine success, you must use your passions. Otherwise, you won't have the drive to push past the hard parts. Many believe that working hard for something you don't care about is called stress, while working hard for something you love is passion.

This chicken or egg debate is challenging to wrap our heads around, but I am going to shed some light on that right now. There is one problem with the way these people define success. A life of passion *is* the success, not something that will carry you to success.

Life of passion = success

We can find passion first and have that carry us towards our goals. For the majority, we stumble upon our passion from following this specific formula. We must combine our who we are, our strengths, relative interests, and ideal environment. Also, having a solid why, which ultimately helps us solve our favorite problems that are greater than our own personal desires.

Finding your passion through finding your favorite hobby works for some, but is not the case for the majority. Bonus points to those who plug in their favorite hobby into their career, but that is not required to live a life of equal or greater passion. Many people have their career of passion and have a favorite hobby that they love on the side. It is healthy to have a balance between the two. There is no right or wrong as this answer varies from person to person. I encourage you to approach creating your passion through the lens of finding your strengths and solving your favorite problem to aid a higher good.

Solving your favorite problem = passion.

You can't wait around for your passion to strike. You may think you want to plan and analyze every career path available for years, because if you make the wrong choice you're stuck. We can feel more trapped by not taking action towards trying new things, as opposed to another person who made the wrong choice and needs to find their passion again.

Step 2: The New You: Unlock Your Potential with Self Honesty

Voluntary Ignorance

We all have problems we think we can't fix, but in reality, we are just resisting change and discomfort in some shape or form.

Ask yourself this question:

What do you know that you wish you didn't know?

This is a harsh reality to face for most. An individual might hide from themselves that they hate their job, but don't want to do anything about it because it scares them. Some people might even wonder if they married the right person, but they don't want to enter the dating scene again. Sometimes people worry about their health, but it scares them to go to the doctor because they do not want to face the reality of a situation. Some may never log into their 401k because they are afraid to find out they don't have enough to retire.

The first step to living your life of freedom and finding your passion is to face whatever reality scares you. The first step to action is knowledge, and action is power that will free you from the shackles of your situation. What gives us pain in the short term, gives us the most beautiful gift in the long term. A great analogy is childbirth. After hours of tremendous pain, the mother is left with her beautiful creation of life.

You may experience great pain by facing your dark truth, but my dear friend, it will all be worth it in the end. Great pain causes significant change, and change is the key to finding your passion.

Gratitude: The Double-Edged Sword

Gratitude is a deeply rewarding skill and habit that I choose to cultivate every day. Even during my worst, I was up before the sun, walking around my neighborhood and reciting my 10 gratitudes for the day. However, gratitude can quickly become a crutch in my experience. We must be ruthlessly honest with ourselves.

Gratitude can't be used as a bypass for our own inner truth.

What does your heart and gut tell you about your situation?

Chances are, since you are holding this book, you are not satisfied with your current life. The first step to healing is to be honest with yourself. Truth above gratitude is the real spiritual practice.

For one of my first jobs, I worked in a grocery store deli. It was honest work and perfect for me during that time of my life. I worked with people there that have been there their whole life. Some loved it, but many did not. I saw a constant theme with these many of these people. They were always trying to go home early and spending enormous amounts of energy working less and make others pick up the slack. They were miserable and hated their jobs, but when I asked them how they felt about their job, they would respond with, "I am so grateful to work at the best paying grocery store."

Okay, so their actions told everyone a different story than the story they verbalized. That is respectable and admirable on the surface level. I too would succumb to using gratitude as my crutch.

I respect their mindset as long as they are being honest with themselves. However, the root of the problem was that they hated working there. Some people love that line of work, while others did not. Everyone is happier when they pair gratitude, honesty, and action towards finding their passion.

Being grateful is still an essential piece to finding your freedom or else you will be miserable. Sometimes that misery is exactly what you need to kick yourself down the rabbit hole of chasing discomfort and the unknown. Being unhappy can be a useful tool, if used correctly. I still highly advise that you recite what you are grateful for in the morning, but follow with brutal compassion and honesty.

Take Radical Responsibility

To summarize people who don't know what they truly love even in their free time fall into one of two categories:

1. They haven't tried that many new activities.
2. They have fallen deep into apathy, complacency, short term thinking, and accepted their fate of unhappiness.

I have been in both categories and I know all too well how it feels. I have deep compassion for those under the spell of victimhood from the bottom of my heart.

The truth is cold and hard for those who don't know what they want to do. They don't know what they want to do because telling themselves that takes away self-responsibility. It takes away the discomfort of action and solidifies our fear of failure. The longer we wait to take action towards finding our purpose, the larger our fear of failure grows. There is no easier time to start than now.

The moment that changed my life was the moment I started taking massive amounts of responsibility. I believe that nothing happens to me, everything happens because of me. Both the good and the not so good.

In 2017, a careless driver with a drunk bachelor party in his car ran a red light and hit me while I was turning on a green arrow. It totaled my 1995 Honda Accord that had 250k miles and smelled like cat piss. (I was very proud of that car, don't make fun of me!)

This left me out of work for 4 months because I had a hard time moving my neck.

The man driving the car lied about running the red

light so his insurance wouldn't have to pay for the damages. Believe it or not, I was more upset about the car because I took a 2-hour public transit ride to work each way for 1.5 years so I could afford it.

The whole situation was my fault. I should have worked harder and planned my time better at my day job, because if I had gotten off earlier, I wouldn't have been in the perfect place to get hit. I am just grateful it wasn't worse.

When I was working minimum wage, I got eaten alive by bedbugs every night in my first apartment. That was my fault for not building high income skills using the internet while going to high school. I was so happy to have the freedom of that apartment, even with the little bed buddies.

The 33k I accumulated in student loans? It was my fault for not applying for more scholarships than I already did. I am just grateful that I didn't leave with more loans.

The 7k in loans from my failed e-commerce business? My fault for underestimating the market and overestimating my skills at the time.

The Coronavirus caused my hours to get cut from my last job. That was my fault because I didn't have a recession-proof side hustle. I met someone online who lost their job and built a sanitization business right after COVID hit. They had no Money, back against a wall, but found an opportunity and took it.

I am by no means saying that I had it rough because I did not. Not even close. Kids in third world countries without water have it rough. Many of my readers have had rougher circumstances. I am blessed beyond belief. I just want to show you my belief system with personal examples to help you make your step towards radical responsibility.

I know my belief system sounds extreme and even ridiculous to some. It is okay if you don't agree with me, but the impact of taking massive responsibility in my life has led to extreme amounts of happiness and fulfillment. Find a belief system that works for you individually, towards taking some responsibility for some things that have happened to you.

Your New Identity

Nothing is wrong with you.

You are exactly where you need to be on your journey right now.

Everything until this point happened for a reason.

You are hungry for passion and will do whatever it takes.

You are strong and worthy of your dream life.

You can do this and as long as you take daily consistent effort, nothing will stop you.

So, take a deep breath and simply focus on the first step...

"The journey of a thousand miles begins with one step."–Lao Tzu

Summary

Being honest with ourselves is the scariest and hardest step in the beginning of our journey. Be patient with yourself and know that facing your problem is the first step that deserves major credit. You have already accomplished more than many will in their entire life. Keep pushing onward because I promise this will get easier.

Action Steps:

- Write down what you know that you wish you didn't know.

- Write down what you are unsatisfied with in your life. Put gratitude aside just for a minute.

- Write down why you are in this life situation. Take full responsibility and be honest with yourself.

Step 3: Unveil Your Techne Skills

Techne is an ancient Greek word for a set of skills that matter to you. You feel driven to work hard on these skills, because they are unique to you and they breathe life into your soul. They allow you to not only serve yourself, but to serve other people. Finding these skills is actually easier than you think.

What do you get compliments on from your friends, family and spouse? Take the Clifton Strengths Assessment from Gallup.com. You can get the test for free when you buy the book Strengths Finder 2.0 by Tom Rath at the time of writing this book.

Yes, it will cost money. Will it be the best money you've ever spent? Yes.

My business communications professor referred this test to me when I was in college. I am forever grateful because it made my fat college bill at the end worth it.

Once you receive your top 5 strengths, then you are better equipped to choose a potential business or career. The answers you receive don't have to be literal, you can read between the lines a little. The greatest satisfaction will come from using your techne skills to help other humans. Once you find your techne skills, ignoring them will be the biggest mistake of your life and starving them will leave you unfulfilled on your death bed. Individuals who find their techne skills and use them to help others are the people changing the world. When you do something nice for somebody, you immediately feel it in your heart. When you see fellow humans struggling and you step in to make their life easier, that is where the real happiness lies. The Strengths Assessment will give you 5 of your best techne skills.

Action Step:

- Take the Clifton Strengths 34 Assessment.

- Or take another test that gives you your top 5 strengths

Reminder: The cheapest way to get the 34 test is by buying the book, *StrengthsFinder 2.0* by Tom Rath. You will pay double the price at the time of writing this book for the 34 test, if you buy the course from their website.

They have a cheaper test called the Clifton 5 Strengths that is the same price of the book on their website, but it does not give you all the information that the 34 Assessment does. Get the redemption code for the 34 from the book.

I am not affiliated with Gallup, or Clifton, and I don't know Tom Rath personally. I just simply can't find a more detailed test online. There is a close second, though. Huge shoutout to my Business Communications professor at Portland Community College for pointing me to that test.

Step 4: Discover What Ignites You

Hobbies vs Potential Careers

Discovering our interests is the easiest first step to finding our passion, but when we make our decision at the end, it will hold the least amount of weight. There is a reason why I am having you find your interests first. Through finding your interests, you will discover who you are and what you like through new experiences. This will eventually lead to you combining all this information and finding your favorite problem to solve.

Be wary about the difference between hobbies and career interests. The goal is not necessarily to find a favorite hobby and then form a career around it. Instead, if a hobby is important, you must form your career around that. The key is not giving your favorite hobby too much weight when making your decision, because you don't want to settle with a career you don't like in favor of a hobby. If you can combine your favorite hobby and career, then I respect that because it works for many, but not the majority. In my research, the majority discover their passion from solving their favorite problem. The goal of finding your interests is to help you solidify your identity of who you are, what you like, don't like and are good at.

This section is very important, because when making career decisions we have to use experience over theory. Many books on passion have people define all this criterion before they even know how to answer the questions. My approach is to help you find the answers instead of making you feel you should already know the answer.

College counselor: "What? You don't know who you are and what you like to do yet? Get to the back of the line. NEXT!" Seriously, that is how I felt at career fairs in college.

We have to apply what we learn from actually doing each activity. The problem with my experience in college is I was never walked through and taught HOW to run a business. They taught me everything you need to know about dated marketing strategies, what legal entity to choose, how to send a formal email, how to give a presentation, and even how to write a business plan.

I asked one of my buddies with a marketing degree to help me with my online ads. They looked at me and said, "Wait, you are actually running online ads? We learned about what they are, but I don't know how to set them up, much less run them." I am sure that this was just a fluke and many of my readers had an exceptional experience in marketing school. My point is, nothing beats application.

Overall, my personal experience with business school was that we talked and theorized about starting a business, even wrote out a business plan, but everything I learned in my two years of college paled compared to what I learned during my first two months of starting my e-commerce store. To be clear, I am not knocking college. College is required for the majority, but for an authorpreneur like me, I found it all bark and no bite. Nothing will replace taking action. Relying on research, hearsay, or expectations over years can become a waste of precious, limited time.

Be an Experience Junkie

Speaking of wasting time, one of the major causes of regret is settling on the first job an individual gets because it is familiar. Would someone marry the first person they had a crush on in middle school? For many of us, that would be a disaster. I am a firm believer that more often than not we need to treat jobs like partners, date around a little to find out what we like and don't like before going all in.

These next 7 exercises must be completed before moving on. Often finding your interest will be reading between the lines, you can take these exercises literally but I would encourage you to keep an open mind.

- Open up a journal or favorite note taking app and brain vomit every interest that comes to mind. Add them to a master list before doing the next exercises.

Exercise 1: Pay Attention to What You Loved as a Child

When you are a child, you feel like anything is possible. You are not worried about failing. In fact, you learn that failing leads to rewards. For example, falling down leads to learning how to walk.

Have you ever lost track of time and felt completely immersed into a task or activity? That could be a clue to lead you closer. For me personally, I used to fall deep into video games as a child. I would lose my sense of self and enjoy being a virtual character and helping virtual people. When I discovered that bettering myself and helping real people feels a million times better than virtually. I fell deeply in love with self-improvement and writing.

I was also obsessed with plastic building block sets. My favorite part about buying a new block set was not building it, but taking it apart and creating something new. Understanding my love for building things directly led to me loving entrepreneurship and building businesses. I was also completely obsessed with geography and maps, this led me to realizing my love for travel.

I am sharing my examples with you to help you brainstorm how you can connect your childhood activities with your techne skills. Turn your analytical mind off when remembering what you used to do as a child. You can't trust your judgements because you have been brainwashed by a society of people believing it's normal to get their energy and joy for life harvested in the name of a 'realistic' future.

Exercise 2: What Do You Constantly Talk About to Your Friends & Loved Ones?

Ask those closest to you what you won't shut up about. Turn off your judgements about how these activities are not sustainable or a career. What you talk about doesn't lie and there is a goldmine of answers here.

Exercise 3: Money Talks

Check your bank statements. What do you spend the most money on? Follow the money, as the money does not lie.

Exercise 4: Search History

Check the search history on your favorite search engine. What do you research the most? This could lead to finding a clue. Remember, don't be too literal about these exercises because the answer often lies between the lines.

Exercise 5: Check Your Social Media

What accounts and hashtags are you following? This is a very underrated tip to discovering what you enjoy. When you notice a post or picture you love, brain storm why you love that post. The

Exercise 6: Why You Love Stories

What are your favorite books, movies and TV shows? Inspect the main characters. I will bet that the reason you love these stories is that you resonate with at least one of the main characters on a deeply personal level. As a kid, I loved Indiana Jones movies and my current favorite fiction book is *The Alchemist* by Paulo Coelho. I love adventure and the art of fulfilling one's purpose in life. Reflect on your favorite stories and you will learn about yourself.

Exercise 7: Resistance vs. Dislike

Sometimes taking the backwards approach is the easiest tactic. Write down everything you don't like to do and be very honest with yourself. Be careful about judging something you don't like too quickly. Something you may have hated in the past could grow into something you love in the future.

One reason that people struggle to find their passion is that they don't give something a second or third try. We rarely enjoy activities we are not good at or we view as hard. Once we get better at this activity, then the passion could spark.

Give everything an honest try. My first-time snowboarding, my friend took me to the top of the mountain instead of teaching me how to stop on the bunny slope. He told me to follow him and before I knew it, we were at the top of the mountain. I asked where's the bunny slope? He took off speeding down the mountain. I had to learn quickly because it was do or fly off the mountain. Once we got to the bottom, I found the slope and practiced stopping, but the fear was already instilled after the first run. I hated and dreaded each run because I felt like I was on the brink of dying. If you are a skier or snowboarder, you may be laughing at me right now, but to me that was terrifying. After a couple more trips, I learned to love snowboarding. The thrill, the wind and beautiful scenery is such a wonder.

As a child, I used to dislike writing papers for school. Now, I love writing and it literally keeps me up all hours of the night sometimes. I learned to approach writing with the perspective of it being a vessel to impact people's lives and a way to express myself creatively. I spent almost a year writing my first book, and as soon as my first review came in; I was addicted to that feeling.

The feedback loop of making the world a better place is addicting. At the time I used to think if my work helped just one person it would make that entire year of working 80 hours a week worth it all. Give each activity an honest try because our brains aren't fully developed until well into the early 20s, according to Dr. Jay Giedd chair of psychiatry at Rady Children's Hospital-San Diego.

There will be some activities you know right off the bat you do not enjoy, especially if you tried them in your mid 20s or after. Write those down now before reading on. Keep an open mind for everything else.

There is one exception. In my experience, the answer won't always be obvious.

activities we have the most resistance to are the activities that we need to do the most. Stephen King says that the first 10 minutes of sitting down to write is like "smelling a dead fish walking into a monkey house." Then he says that something will click and that leads to something else. Soon he can't help himself. He wants to skip meals, and has to force himself to stop.

You might not enjoy most activities you try. Welcome to the club. It is impossible to know if you'll like something if you never try it, so get out there! Take out a piece of paper and write down everything that you think you might even remotely enjoy. Try not to judge and write them all down. You may notice resistance towards certain activities that you write down. Usually those are the ones that you need to try most. Impromptu public speaking? Sign me up.

Prioritize your list from the most resistance to the least resistance. I know this might sound counterintuitive, but sometimes the activities you have an interest in come with high internal resistance. This is a signal that the activity could become the most rewarding and fulfilling because it requires you to change for the better.

You Killed Curiosity

Have you ever bought books before that have just sat around the house going unread? Have you ever felt like you can't buy more books unless you finish the ones you bought? This makes sense from a minimalist or financial aspect; however, I highly suggest that you don't turn a fun hobby into a chore. The same thing happens when we watch video streaming apps but start adding more videos to our "watch later" playlist than we actually end up watching. Soon this list will feel like something you have resistance to do because the idea of finishing it is overwhelming.

When you force yourself to do something that is supposed to be fun then you can accidentally kill the fun. Follow your current curiosity, even if it changes a lot. You are the cat and you are killing your curiosity.

Summary

Once you have your master list fully complete, organize them from the most resistance you feel to the least resistance you feel. Schedule a day once a week to try the interest you have the most resistance to. This is to help build your confidence and tolerance for discomfort. Your gut reaction might be to try to ignore my advice by not doing the most resisted interest. If that is the case then you are not ready to change. You will only be ready to change once the pain from a mediocre life becomes greater than the pain of doing that most resisted activity.

Action Steps:

- Take out a piece of paper and brain vomit all your potential interests. This is your master interest list.

- Go through exercise 1-7 and write down your interests. Write down everything that comes to mind and don't worry about it being related to a career or not yet.

- Reorganize your list from most resistance to least resistance.

- Put a star next to the interests that could be a potential career. For some of these, it will be hard to know until you try it.

- Plan a time when you will pursue your most resisted interest.

- Finish the whole list by doing 1 new interest every 2 weeks. This will take time, so patience is key.

Step 5: Define & Design Your Dream Environment

Exercise 8: Reverse Lifestyle Design: The Holy Grail of Finding Fulfillment

Grab a piece of paper or open a writing application. This exercise is the sword on your conquest for happiness. This exercise is the backwards approach to finding your career. The way you were taught to find your career is the exact opposite way to find career fulfillment. Many of us chose our careers because it was secure, safe, realistic, and pays well. Treat this exercise with respect because it is the single most helpful exercise. I've used it to find my own dream life. Take all your preconceived notions of how to find your dream and throw them in the garbage disposal.

If money or time was not an issue, what would your ideal day look and feel like exactly?
Write down what you would do down to the little detail.

Don't worry about defining what should be leisure or work yet. Throw your filters out the window and write down your fantasy. Be completely honest with yourself because the answer will lie between the lines. It's so funny because many people who don't know what they love usually write sleeping, or Watching TV shows as their passion.

The truth is, the reason they love sleep is because their energy is being sucked from your current lifestyle. Once they remove that activity out of the equation, I guarantee you nobody will be wishing they could sleep their life away once they discover how glorious it can be. Once you find your genuine passion, it will keep you up late at night and wake you up early in the morning because you can't wait to get back to it. That is genuine passion. I must note that the passionate person does not intend to miss sleep it just happens sometimes. Your new problem will be focusing deeper on your work so you can sleep more.

Sleep, ironically, is a profession that many people are passionate about. If that is the case then you can apply to be a professional bed tester as that is a legitimate profession. If an individual truly loves watching TV shows, then maybe your passion is being in the film industry in some way. Maybe finding a job or business where you can talk, write or be involved somehow in the media industry is the best option. There is no right or wrong answer. I am willing to bet that if money, time, or energy was not the issue, then our ideal days would differ completely from our current days.

Start with the first thing that you feel and do in the morning. Here are some questions that you can use to write your ideal day exercise.

- Where would you wake up?
- How would you feel? Would you hit snooze on the alarm clock?

- What would your morning routine look like?
- Who would you be with?
- What flavors would you taste?
- What are your friends like?
- What activities would you do?
- Where would you watch the sunset?

Be very specific and again hold nothing back. When doing this exercise, I've had some people tell me that they want to drink beer on the beach all day. This answer is blunt, honest and hilarious. I love it! Most likely this will be an after-work activity that they can build their work around. If you have a dream though, who am I to tell someone they can't do it? I told them that pursuing some form of passive income would be a possible long-term option. As well as being a beer tester in an exotic location or even building a business around beer. It is not anyone's place to judge a person's passion.

When doing this exercise ask yourself, what answers would your inner child say?

For most people your after-work passions will differ from your work passions, take this exercise with a grain of salt. An effective part of the passionate life recipe is having a symbiotic relationship between your work life and after-work passions.

Sometimes solving your work-related passion is easier once you find your ideal lifestyle. For example, the reason I got into finding online jobs was because I wanted the freedom to work from anywhere and to make my own schedule.

Finally, when you finish this exercise, put it in a safe place and read it to yourself every morning and night. This might sound ridiculous, but it will solidify your "why", which we will discuss in a later chapter.

Hunt Down Your Tribe

There are thousands of people who are hardworking, self-independent and living the exact life that you desire. Use the information from your ideal day to find the people who are already living your dream.

When I found the people living my dream life, I almost didn't believe it. So, I got on a plane and flew across the world to meet them. Many people, including my past coworkers, assumed that all these people are trust fund babies. I am telling you if you look hard enough, you will find your tribe of self-made hard-working professionals no matter what your desired field is.

What did they have to do to get there?

What exactly are these people doing for a living?

Do one of these jobs align with your techne skills, interests, who you are and who you want to become?

If you woke up in their shoes, would you enjoy your new daily life?

Just keep in mind that people usually make what they do appear easier or more fun than it actually is on social media. There is no free lunch in life and everything has to be attained through deep focus.

The moment that absolutely changed my life and pulled me out of the pits of hopelessness was when I discovered the "Travel Like a Boss" podcast. The host of this amazing show interviews hard-working people who are remote employees, entrepreneurs and freelancers who form their careers around their love for travel. As long as these people have an internet connection, the entire world is open to them. Each episode is about an hour long and goes deep into how each person got their lifestyle.

Browse your favorite podcast app and find a podcast that interviews people who do what you love daily and you will discover a new fire for life.

Ideal Workplace Environment

When figuring out whether a career is right for you, take into consideration the work environment, hours, your boss, and colleagues. This step is often overlooked, but heavily affects your overall happiness.

Do you want to work for a big international company? Do you want to help pioneer a small startup? Do you want to start your own company and be your own boss?

What hours and days do you want to work?

Do you want to work from home or remotely?

Do you like variety or do you like doing the same thing every week?

Do you want to be in control of your work load?

How many hours a week do you want to work for a healthy work life balance?

The answer to this question varies depending on your values and what responsibilities you have in life. In my early twenties, I found that I could balance a social life easily with a 40 to 60-hour work week. I would cycle with spurts of 80-hour work weeks for 3 months on and 1 month back to 40-60 hours just to keep some level of sanity. During these 80-hour work weeks, I would go full monk mode. When I wasn't working, I would walk in mindfulness, meditate, and visualize.

I found the most effective way to combat burnout was to do nothing in my free time, just sitting in silence and breathing. If I filled my free time with stimulus, then my work hours would have diminished returns. I go in depth on my burnout recovery journey in my new book, *The Art of Doing Nothing: The No-Guilt Practical Burnout Recovery System for Busy Professionals.*

What values do you want your coworkers to share with you?

This question is often overlooked and can easily spoil an otherwise perfect career. When you feel part of a team, all working towards accomplishing something worthwhile yet challenging, then you could find your spark.

What do you value in a leader?

The right manager can make or break the otherwise perfect job of your dreams. I know you are all too familiar with this. The best way to learn what you like and don't like is to reflect on your experiences.

Summary

Once you define your ideal environment it makes finding your dream life infinitely easier. Be specific as possible when defining what environment you want. The more specific, the more likely you will find a way to make it happen. It also ensures that you don't enter another career that wasn't what you expected. Being specific with what you want makes it infinitely easier to receive what you desire. Once you find your tribe of people all on the same mission with the same desires, then your dream solidifies as real in your mind. I require this step before moving on, because if you don't believe then you won't achieve or receive.

Action Steps:

- Write down in full detail your answer to Exercise 9: Reverse Lifestyle Design. Aim for 1 to 2 pages at least.

- Go to your favorite video streaming app and a search engine to find the people living your dream life. Spend 20 minutes a day combing through channels, articles, blogs and interviews until you find them.

- Write down exactly what you want out of your dream job.

Step 6: Bonus Hacks to Discover Yourself

Exercise 9: Highlight of the Day

Pay close attention to what lights you up while living your current life. At the end of every day get into the habit of writing the 1 thing that you did or happened to you that made your day.
It doesn't matter what it is. It can be that cute person you met waiting in line to get coffee or that colleague at work that you helped. That project you managed or that meeting that went well. Write it down. When you find moments of inspiration, this exercise will make it easier to understand why you felt inspired and how you can replicate that feeling.

The Fastest Way to Collect Experiences

Nothing, absolutely nothing in this world will teach you more than traveling. I am not just saying that because I am discovering my love for travel. Traveling has literally opened my mind to how endless our possibilities are.

I thought I had a colorful spectrum of experiences under my belt until I went to Thailand. The people I met, the strange street food I ate, the spontaneous activities I tried and the perspective I received was worth 100-fold what I spent on the trip. The memories I have and the lessons I learned will stick with me for the rest of my life.

What scares me even more is to think I almost didn't go because of many excuses. I didn't feel like the time was right. I didn't feel like I had enough money or time because I had student loans and was working 80 hours a week just to lose more money from my business. I ate plain brown rice, ground turkey and spinach all day every day for 5 years so I could save money to travel. I threw all my excuses aside and requested the time off from my day job and booked my ticket. The lessons I learned from that trip ended up paying me back in ways I never could have imagined.

Now you may wonder, am I suggesting that you do the same? No. My advice is to always pay off debt and get an emergency fund before traveling. However, we must also remember the resource that we are spending whether or not we travel and that is TIME. The inspiring people I met and the lessons I learned on that trip gave me the confidence to pivot literally everything about my life. I changed my job and my business model, but more importantly, I changed from the inside out. The 1k I spent on that 2-week trip was my tuition for the school of life, and I would gladly enroll again with extra honor courses.

For most, a weeklong trip is the most realistic option and I realize even that could be a stretch, but the benefits will outweigh the negatives if planned properly.

Start a bucket list of places you want to go and

then plan a 1-2 week-long trip once you are ready, you will not regret it.

Changing Scenery for Maximum Growth

The next level life hack to grow and change quickly is to move to a new city, state or even country. If you are in a position of independence and don't have to be there for immediate family, then this could be one of the most beneficial actions you could take for your life. The sheer amount of growth by trial-and-error skyrockets when you move to a strange city or country.

A study by Adam Galinsky, a professor at Columbia Business School, found that those who have lived abroad are more creative. He even found that the more countries an individual lived in, the more creative their career choice tended to be. Galinsky stated that being a tourist does not record much of a benefit. He says, "Someone that lives abroad and doesn't engage with the local culture will likely get less of a creative boost than someone who travels abroad and really engages in the local environment."

Another interesting study conducted by Dr. Julia Zimmermann and Dr. Franz suggests that travel can be linked to personality development and the way we interact with people. They compared a large sample of German University students who had studied abroad for at least a semester with another group who haven't traveled before.

The study showed that the group who studied

abroad were higher in extraversion than the group that didn't travel. When the study abroad students returned home, they were recorded having a higher likelihood to be open to new experiences, agreeable, and emotionally stable.

Traveling also helps us keep a sharp mind according to a study commissioned by the U.S. Travel Association. The act of figuring out how to do simple tasks, in a strange environment, such as taking public transit and ordering food, sharpens the mind.

I am not suggesting this as necessarily a viable option for you. Believe me, I realize this is easier said than done. Make the call if this is appropriate for you. Who knows, if you find a career you're passionate about somewhere else in the world, then you might want to give moving a shot!

Try Other Jobs Within Your Company

If switching companies feels like drudgery, sometimes the easier, more short-term solution is to try a new position in your current company. This is the dip your toe in method and it's a viable approach to changing your life. Sometimes all it takes is a tiny step to propel you into a world of change. If you already have a solid reputation within your company, then it's easier and more comfortable to make the switch. Instead of just jumping into a new role, it pays to talk to people in your desired roll first.

Summary

Overall, these hacks are extremely helpful tools to keep in your arsenal but are not required to find your life of passion. If traveling is out of the question for now, then talk to people who have other jobs in your company that you have an interest in.

Action Steps

- Identify if there is a position in your company that you want to try. If so, find someone with that position and talk to them tomorrow during your work day.

- Keep a notepad of highlights from your day. Before bed write them down.

- Plan a self-growth travel trip. If not now, then 5 years from now.

Step 7: The Biggest Secret to Unlock Unlimited Motivation

Define Your Philanthropic Why

The secret to unleashing motivation and igniting passion into your life is **finding your why.** The reason why you do challenging tasks. The reason that makes all those early mornings and late nights worthwhile. This chapter is all about why you must define not only your personal why but also your philanthropic why.

When your why is larger than yourself, you unlock a whole new level of determination and drive. According to a Professor Adam Grant of Wharton Management, "doing work that affects the wellbeing of others" and meeting the people affected by their work is very motivating for employees.

In an experiment conducted by the University of Michigan, they assigned cold callers to find scholarship money for students in need. The cold callers that spent time with the student could bring in 171% more money on average when compared to the cold callers who didn't meet the student. The act of meeting the person in need and connecting with them on a person level boosted the performance of the fundraiser. The key I believe, is to start small. If you are struggling to find passion in your current situation, then find the customers or employees that you are helping if possible. This simple act could breathe a whole new life into your career or give you an idea of what you want in the future.

My biggest passion and what drives everything I do is obtaining freedom. True freedom of time and location independence. That is great and all, but my real why is helping those who don't have freedom and can't escape. I donate a portion of my earnings to child labor and human trafficking victims, because I feel a deep sense of urgency and a burning desire to free those who are trapped.

I write books about freeing the time and minds of my readers so I can help my fellow humans achieve their own version of freedom. For me, striving to help as many people as possible achieve internal and external freedom wakes me up at 3 am to write.

To find your deep and burning why, think back to giant obstacles that you have overcome and how good it made you feel when you achieved it. It doesn't have to be grandiose, the best why's are often the most simplistic. Just remember that you will never regret altruism.

The passion might not strike immediately in the beginning the same way that your favorite hobby does. Sometimes to get that strong feeling of your career being your passion, you have to see the results of your work affecting the lives of others.

That is acceptable because what we like to do does not always align with what we are good at. Do not wait for your passion to strike. Take action towards finding how you can give value back to the world. Blend in your skills, ideal work environment, with knowing yourself and paying attention to the results. Bonus points if you initially have interest in the work that you are doing before the passion strikes.

What Are Your Goals?

Will this new career give you what you want out of life? You have to be willing to make compromises here. For me personally I want to retire my grandma. I know that if I keep focusing on solving people's problems, then it will be possible. I want to help her the same way she helped me my entire life. You have to be honest with yourself, what goals would make you happier if you accomplished them?

The biggest key to figuring out if a goal is worthwhile is asking yourself this simple question.

Instead of "can I do this?", ask yourself, "how can I *not* do this?

Your why has to be so strong that it feels second nature to you. It can be as simple as having more free time to watch your children grow up.
Tony Robbins knew he wanted to buy an island for his mom, so he made it happen. I am not saying that you need to be rich to be happy. That is far from true, but using your fortune to help others is a very motivating why.

Many entrepreneurs and busy professionals at the end of their life often regret how much time they spent on work. Some people value Lamborghinis and owning the biggest mansion in the world. If that is your gig, then more power to you. These are not necessarily bad goals, but they won't lead to your happiness in the long term or be a powerful enough why. The skills that an individual learns from the journey of obtaining enough money to buy a Lambo is the real prize. The Lambo would be the cherry on top to a much higher purpose.

No one can tell you the right answer. The goal of this section is to help you become a long-term thinker.

Can your career lead to accomplishing a big goal that would increase your happiness?

Find a way for your career to help you accomplish your relationship, financial, social, and personal development goals for maximum joy.

Finding Your Personal Why: What is Important to You

Think about times in the past where you took massive action towards a change in your life.

Why did you make that change? Why did you go through that struggle?

When you feel you have to do something you just do it. When you feel you "should" do something, then you encounter resistance induced paralysis. You found your why and everything else became irrelevant. Examples include breakups, moving locations, starting a new good habit or quitting a bad habit.

When there is resistance to do something you supposedly want to do, then there are one of two culprits.

1. Don't have a strong enough why or reason to doing or stopping that activity.
2. You feel you have to do it because of some external force, person or circumstance.

When finding your why you have to use these questions to pin down the specifics.

1. What will happen if I don't take this action?
2. What is not having this scenario costing me?
3. What will happen if I do this behavior?
4. How will it make me feel when I do/don't do this behavior?
5. What will my life look and feel like when I do/don't do this behavior?

Write down your answers to these questions. When you doubt the journey but know in your gut that you need to keep pushing. The answer is to find your why. Keeping pushing on, you beautiful soul.

Action Steps:

- Write down exactly what your 10, 5 and 1-year goals are.

- Go over your strengths and try to brain storm what potential problems you could solve with your skill set.

- The 34 Strengths Assessment gives you ideas For jobs and problems you like to solve.

- Refer back to your childhood interests to help discover your favorite problems.

- Write down your personal why. Use the goals you defined and take them a step deeper. Why do you want to accomplish these goals?

- **Write down your philanthropic why.** Be as detailed as possible. The most important part of this exercise is to identify why you want to solve this problem. If this philanthropic why doesn't stick, then your Personal why will help you find your philanthropic why.

Step 8: Validating Your Genuine Passion

A study done in 2019 by the nonprofit group Mental Health America and the FAAS Foundation found that out of 17,000 U.S. workers in 19 different industries, 71% said that they are looking to change employers. The good news is you are not alone. The bad news is you will be one of the 71% until you find your life of passion. You may not find your genuine passion on the first go, statistics show. Take some pressure off yourself and know that you don't have to perfect. Don't be one of the Sheep. Be the wolf that never gives up.

Use this exercise below to help validate if the passion you want to pursue is your genuine passion. When you answer these questions, try to put yourself into the shoes of your future self in your new career.

Exercise 10: Your Future Self

- Who are you?
- What do you do?
- What do you feel supremely qualified to teach people to do?
- Who do you do it for?
- What do they want or need from you?

- How do these people change as you give them this result?

When you go to a scholarly reunion or professional networking event, you are always asked "so what do you do?" Alas, this question never stops even when you grow up! This is a very peculiar question because if you answer with what you love to do in your free time, you are immediately met with them asking for you to specify what you do for work. It's like telling people what you love to do is not enough. They mainly want to know about your profession. If you don't know what to tell people, then give them the simple answer from question 6.

I have some colleagues that write children's books. When asked what they do for a living, they describe how they help children across the world fall asleep so they can have wonderful dreams.

Get creative with your answer and your questioner will wonder what to say after. Instead of asking them about what they do for a living, follow up with, "what are you passionate about?" That will shift the conversation for the better.

Go to Meetup Groups for Your Potential Passions

On your journey of striving for a better life, you may often feel alone. I know I did. I couldn't talk about my search for passion to my coworkers at my last job because they would shut me down, judge, or even discourage me.

One of my most respected colleagues who I looked

up to professionally seriously let me down. I confided in him about my journey pursuing e-commerce and how I wanted to be a full-time entrepreneur one day. He told me he too tried to become an entrepreneur; until he had to make a 401k and health care benefits plan for his employees. He gave up because it was too hard. He told me that being an entrepreneur wasn't worth it because it was too challenging. Since I was so young At the time and I looked up to him for advice within the company, I felt discouraged.

Now I wouldn't give someone else's opinion the time of day unless it aligned with my values.

I grew close to my supervisor at my last job as well. I told her about these people on video streaming websites who were making passive income through different business ventures. She told me that stuff "doesn't seem real". Now, are these people wrong for having these opinions? Of course not, they were simply projecting their reality onto me.

Despite their obvious discontentment, if anyone talked about leaving and pursuing a passion, everyone would start telling them why they were making a mistake. "There are few jobs out there with benefits as good as this one," "There are few jobs out there as secure as this one," or "never leave here, you will regret it." You may experience unhappy people being threatened by you.
I am bringing up this personal encounter because I want to stress the importance of finding a support system of people on a similar journey to you. When I found my tribe of like-minded people at an entrepreneurship conference in Thailand, it became infinitely easier to accomplish my dream.

Find meet ups from social media groups and attend events from meetup websites. This is the ninja hack for sustaining your motivation on your journey to passion. Go speak to the group members and see if you could imagine yourself in their shoes.

When you get to these meet ups you must ask yourself, do you feel you belong?

What do you like or dislike about these people?

At the very least you will find ideas for potentially other activities you can try for your new passion. The key is to talk to people in person who are doing the activities you are interested in.

Making a Living or Making a Life?

Many people choose a career because it will lead to them living a life of security, comfort and prosperity. Those are reasonable goals that we can achieve in many careers. That is not a good enough criterion to choose a career though and is where we run into trouble.

With the cost of universities being so high, we want to make the wisest choice. Many of us feel pressured from our family and high school counselors to go to a university and with that comes an enormous price tag. In order to not be a "failure" we need to go to a university and to be responsible we need to make the cost worth it. So, we choose the degree that will land us the most secure and high-paying job. On the top-level appearance, that seems like an intelligent choice. However, choosing a lifelong career is daunting for an 18-year-old kid fresh out of high school or a knowledgeable worker who is fed up with their current field.

The challenge of deciding what to do can become more difficult when responsibilities pile up. A spouse who relies on you or expects a certain way of life. Children or financial obligations such as a luxury car and grand home. It may feel you are carrying the world on your shoulders. Do not fret. There are ways to simplify and maximize your time to help you get more time to find your passion.

One of the biggest ways I saved time and money was meal prepping for 4 days at a time and only cooking foods that can be cooked fast or on autopilot. I would spend 1 hour cooking every 4 days and yes, that included clean up. The food I ate was not glamorous and would sometimes get boring when eaten all day every day, but the time and money savings were massive. I can always cook ground meat super-fast along with broccoli. Brown rice, baked veggies, and slow cooker recipes are easy autopilot meals to cook. While the food is cooking, you can set a timer and complete other tasks.

Another great time saving hack is to listen to podcasts, interviews or research for your potential interests or careers while you are driving to work or in the shower.

The Solitude Solution

It doesn't matter if you are 18 and trying to decide what you want to do with your life or if you are a knowledgeable worker with a family. Spending time alone will be one of the biggest keys to figuring out who you are and what you love to do.

The way you go about finding time for solitude will vary, but the importance is the same. With no external influences trying to guide your decisions, what do you want to do with your time?

A 10-day silent passion retreat would be ideal but is not necessarily realistic for the busy professional. Arranging 1 day or even a weekend where you can be alone is more than enough.

If you have children, you can pay someone to watch your kids for the weekend. Or you can cut a deal with your spouse to watch them for just 1 weekend while you grab a cabin in the mountains. In return, you could make it up to them by having a special date night or doing a fun new activity.

I know this may seem challenging, but as long as you explain the importance of using this alone time to find your passion to your spouse, then you will have an easier time getting the help to make it happen.

When you are alone how do you feel about yourself?

More money, fame, or power is nothing without a solid self-esteem base. Helping people will make you feel amazing about yourself. Feeling like a badass who accomplishes anything you want will make you feel incredible about yourself.

When you are alone, go through this series of questions:

1. How do I feel about myself?
2. What do I love about myself?
3. What do I love to do for others?
4. What do I value about the work that I do?

Exercise 11: Find Your Values

If You Had 5 Years Left to Live What Would You Do?

This is a profound and invigorating exercise when approached with the right mindset. If you walked into the doctor's office and they told you, "you only have 5 years left to live", what would be your first thought? How would you spend the rest of your life? Palliative nurses counsel the dying during their last weeks. It is strange how our mind sets shift once we approach death.

Bronnie Ware is an Australian author who has spent several years as a palliative nurse. She says that near the end of their lives people have an astonishing clarity of what happened and how they feel about it. Studies show that people on their deathbed rarely have regrets of things they did, it's usually actions they didn't do that torment them until the end.

One of the most common regrets of men is "I wish

I didn't work so much". People also often regret not living a life true to themselves and instead living a life trying to sustain expectations of loved ones or impressing friends and colleagues. People often wish that they had the courage to express their feelings. Many people stuff their feelings down to keep the peace, as a result they feel resentful. The last most common regret is people wish that they let themselves be happier. They stayed in their comfort zones because the overwhelming feelings of taking that opportunity felt too strong to handle.

Fear of change is also a big reason people never pursue what makes them happy. They held a smile on the outside while they held deep dissatisfaction on the inside. They yearned to feel free, laugh deeply, stay in touch with old friends, and pursue what made them happy. There is so much we can learn from these regrets.

I choose to look at myself in the mirror and live every day as if it's my last. Okay, live today as if it's your last within reason. Racking up your credit card with 5-star resorts and skydiving sessions may not be the wisest decision.

Life is too short to not be happy. Approach that cute person at the grocery store, call your long-lost friends, make time for your family, pursue the activities that make you feel alive and help others relentlessly as if your life depends on it, because it does!

Summary

I understand that it can be super challenging to know whether or not what you are pursuing is your passion. Putting yourself in the shoes of your future self is the best place to start. Understanding your intentions with your future career is the next best step and finally understanding our mortality will often make your values clear.

Action Steps:

- Perform exercise 10: your future self.

- Define your exact intentions with this new life. How will your life change with this new purpose?

- Plan a day to be alone. Talk to whoever you have to, to make it happen. Set yourself up to detach from work and family obligations for just one day. Go deep into nature for bonus points.

- Leave your phone in the car and spend your day walking and contemplating your life purpose. This might be painful, but trust me this is required.

- Write down every thought that comes to mind about your life. Getting this information out of your head will help you organize your thoughts.

Step 9: The Well Calculated Leap of Faith

Now that you know your strengths, interests, your why, favorite problem and have some validation, you can solidify down your options and make a choice. Collect your answers to the below questions in one place so you can understand how to decide.

- Narrow down your strengths to the top 3.

- Exercise 8: reverse lifestyle design

- Your ideal work environment

- Exercise 9: highlights of the day

- Exercise 10: your future self

- Notes from your day in solitude

- Exercise 11: your values

- Define your #1 philanthropic why

- Define your #1 personal why

- Define your top 3 favorite problems to solve

- Define your top 3 interests. Do these interests fit inside of your career or after work life?

Keep your selections at 3 or lower because we are trying to prevent information overload, paralysis by analysis, and decision fatigue.

Analyze what your life would be like if you chose those careers. The reason I am having you choose 3 interests is because most of these interests will be hobbies you enjoy doing in your free time.

Your passion career will be a blend of these answers. I ordered them from 1, the most important to 11, the least important.

Design 3 potential careers that are a blend of all of 11 answers. The reason we narrow down your selection down to 3 choices is because we are trying to prevent decision fatigue and analysis paralysis from too many decisions. We need to narrow down everything as much as possible. Pursuing and discovering your interests is one of the most important pieces to the puzzle of finding your career, despite not carrying the most weight for your decision.

Quiet your logical mind and tap into your intuitive side when analyzing your careers. Follow your gut because your first reaction is usually correct, and I have the science to prove it.

Author of *Emotional Intelligence* and Psychologist Daniel Goleman says that "the wisdom of emotions is a real thing." There is part of your brain way down the base of your brain called the basal ganglia, which summarizes all the emotions you have felt based on your experiences. The downside is the basal ganglia doesn't communicate with the prefrontal cortex or other parts of your brain that form communication. Instead, it is connected to your GI tract and limbic system so it gives you information through felt sensations. That is why we get that "gut feeling" that we can't explain.

Start crossing the 3 careers one by one until you get a feeling in your stomach that something is wrong. That might be the career that you need to pursue.

Spend some time alone to meditate on your choice. Walk yourself mentally through your daily life for each career. When you slow your mind down, you can cut the fat and focus on your feelings about the potential decision.

Burning the Ships, FOMO, & Paralysis by Analysis

Fomo is an acronym for the fear of missing out.

Sometimes when people are afraid of not finding their passion, they will choose too many passions to follow at once. Bill Burnet is the executive director for the lifestyle design program of Stanford University. He says that he often has students come into his office during office hours and tell him they are pursuing 3 majors and 2 minors. He suggests to his students that they should "let go and move on".

On the flip side, when people have too many choices at their immediate disposal, they have what psychologists call "choice overload". Studies show that the more options we have, the more likely we won't decide at all. This is most likely because we are afraid of making the wrong decision.

Let go and accept your choice. Remember that nothing is set in stone. Worst-case scenario, you will learn tremendously from all your mistakes. However, there is an advantage to committing fully to your decision that can't be ignored.

A historical decision-making study replicated by Harvard Psychologist Dan Gilbert shows that when we have to decide, we are less happy with the outcome.

Dr. Gilbert conducted a study at Harvard where he created a photography course and invited students to take 12 pictures of their favorite things around Harvard. Then he asked them to choose their top two preferred pictures. From these 2 pictures he asked the students which one they would like to give up to the class as evidence of their project.

Half of the students were informed that if they changed their decision anytime over the next 4 days, they could exchange the one picture they chose for the other picture. The other half was told that they had to make the final decision on the Spot, because the other picture would be sent away to England. He asked the students to predict if they would be happy with their choice.

Dr. Gilbert found that the students who were given a choice to reverse their decision did not like the choice they made, while the group that made the final decision was happy with their choice. He replicated this study but gave the students a heads-up that they could be in the final decision group or the altering decision group. 66% of the students all wanted to have the option to turn their picture in, but that ultimately led to their dissatisfaction with their choice.

According to Dr. Gilbert, the potential to change our minds on a decision makes it harder for us to be content with our decision. Stories throughout history demonstrate how fully committing to a decision will make us more likely to succeed.

In 1519, Captain Hernan Cortes, Spanish explorer and Conquistador landed on the shores of the Yucatan to seize the treasure of the Aztecs. Despite his 500 soldiers, 100 sailors and 11 ships, he was still extremely outnumbered by the enormous 600-year-old Aztec empire. Cortez got wind of some soldiers trying to escape the battle out of uncertainty for victory.

He caught the ring leaders and gave the order to have his men burn their own ships. They all wondered how they would get home with the treasure without their ships. He told them, "If we are going home, we are going home in their ships." After that, it raised the commitment of the men to a whole new level, which led to their victory.

Napoleon Hill in his book, "Think and Grow Rich" tells the story of a man named Edwin C. Barnes who decided he was going to work with one of the greatest inventors on earth, Thomas Edison. No matter what Edison thought of the matter, Edwin knew it would make it happen.

He had no money, no tech skills, and only had the clothes on his back. He made the commitment to himself that he would make his dream come true. In 1905 Barnes used the last of the money he had to his name to buy a freight train ticket to see Edison.

Even though he had ragged clothes because he spent all of his money on the ticket, the midwestern man walked into Edison's laboratory beaming of confidence. He told the famous inventor that he had come to form a partnership with him. Edison's staff watched amused before bursting into hysterical laughter. Edison looked into his eyes and did not laugh as he saw a young man that would do anything necessary to accomplish his dream.

Impressed by his confidence, Edison gave him a job as a floor sweeper. A far cry from being business partners. Barnes swept the floors for years and paid close attention to how Edison worked. Once Edison finished the Epiphone voice recorder, his sales team seemed skeptical of the practicality of his invention. Barnes grabbed the opportunity by making a sales plan for Edison, he agreed to give exclusive distribution rights to Barnes to sell and distribute the voice machine. Barnes ended up selling thousands of machines and became a young millionaire who helped change how the country ran.

History shows that not only will we be happier if we don't have an option to reverse a decision, but we will raise the amount of action it takes to complete our goal. We have to be 100% committed to what we do or not do it at all, because we will waste time and energy. Being under pressure creates traction the same way you need pressure to stand firmly on a steep roof. If you are light-footed, then you lose traction and slip off the roof.

This does not mean that you have to be committed to the same career your whole life. This means that whatever career you choose has to be your 100% commitment while you are doing it.

By no means do I want you to take this advice literally. I don't want you to prevent yourself from deciding because you are worried about not being able to retreat. I suggest that if you make your decision harder to reverse, studies show you will be happier and more satisfied with your choice. With that being said, please don't walk into the CEO's office of your company and make a scene because you are "burning the ships".

Abolishing the Sunk Cost Fallacy

Many people feel like they have to keep pursuing a career or degree they hate because they have spent too much time and money trying to achieve it already. I totally understand how that feels. I spent a good amount of money and time pursuing a business administration degree. I found the degree because I knew from the Strengths Assessment that I loved building things and solving people's problems.

Alas, the closer I got to finishing my degree, the more I discovered that many people in my chosen field are depressed and going through divorces from working 100 hours a week. I realized that my personal fate would be similar, so I dropped out and ate the price tag. I could have finished my degree, but instead of giving into the sunk cost fallacy, I pulled myself out and I am tremendously grateful that I did.

I know that before you chose your dream career; I told you about burning the ships and how people use that to their advantage. There are no black and white answers. I am here to display the whole toolbox to you and help you choose the tool that fits your project the best.

On my journey to discovering my passion, I realized that I needed to know when to throw in the towel or keep pressing on. Knowing the difference is a delicate balance and fine art.

I aggressively pursued an online e-commerce business selling meditation supplies. I worked 80 hours a week total, 40 at my day job and 40 on my business for 3 years. In the end, I had a net loss as I told you earlier. I kept pushing harder and harder and throwing more money into the business, desperate to fix it until one day it dawned on me. I needed to stop throwing money at my problems and find a career where I enjoy solving the problems more.

Overall, I was not happy pursuing this business, and I needed to find a more fulfilling business model. If you are struggling with knowing if you should keep pushing forward, then I highly recommend this book by Seth Godin called *The Dip*. This is the book that inspired me to pivot business ventures and to dig deeper into my next one. The book won't tell you to quit or pursue anything, but it will definitely lead you to making your own conclusion in the name of finding your genuine passion.

We all must be wary of "shiny object syndrome", on the contrary. We can't spend all of our time chasing the newest career, but when it gets hard, we pivot to the next popular business model. Finding a career or business and taking the initial steps is the fun, straightforward part.

Once the challenge sets in and our skills are tested, that's when we face the real decision. We need to know when to call it quits because sticking to a career we hate will not only result in our own suffering but the suffering of our close relationships. When we are miserable, we often are not a pleasure to be around and that will put a strain on our relationships.

There is an art to knowing when to keep fighting and when to know enough is enough. We will always have dips or struggles in any venture that we do. This is normal and not a sign that we should quit. However, if you have been giving your best for a while and you are not happy, then you must reevaluate the reason why you are pursuing this journey.

Drop Expectations

Expectations can crush the joy of your journey. You may be thinking, but Chandler, you painted this glorious picture of how my life of passion will be heaven on earth. This is not how my passion started out. I chose my well calculated career, crushed by initial resistance, grew my skills, found my why and then had the spark of passion explode into my life like a nuke.

Keep in mind that when you see your friends talk about their passion on social media understand that the grass always looks greener on the other side. Shiny object syndrome is an actual condition where an individual becomes very good at many activities but excels at none. When you focus on your one thing then you will achieve mastery which will lead to more passion. Do not confuse this with settling. If I didn't pivot my last life and business, you would not be reading this book.

Summary

Nobody can make the decision for you. Asking for advice or seeking answers from external places will only result in more confusion. You know deep down what you have to do. Once you define your options the answer will lie deep within your gut, in the fiber and essence of your very being. Be patient with yourself, calm your mind and the answer will display itself to you. Once you feel the answer and it aligns with your logical mind, you will know it clear as day.

Action Steps:

- Collecting all your notes from the action steps.

- Narrow down your strengths to the top 3

- Exercise 8: Reverse Lifestyle Design

- Your ideal work environment

- Exercise 9: highlights of the day

- Exercise 10: your future self

- Notes from your day in solitude

- Exercise 11: your values

- Define your #1 philanthropic why

- Define your #1 personal why

- Define your top 3 favorite problems to solve

- Define your top 3 interest for work

- Blend the above 10 criteria to create 3 potential career paths.

- As you check off each career, clear your logical mind and pay attention to your gut.

- Drop expectations

- Commit 100% to mastering your wonderful new career. Burn the ships?

Step 10: Taking Massive Action

You found something that you enjoy most of the time? Congratulations! You put in the work to try new things and you deserve the credit for chasing discomfort. If you spread your energy and time too thin, then you won't have enough time to get good at it. Your passion usually increases for activities you are good at. So as discussed, the activity you love now will only grow sweeter with age, just like an exquisite red wine, but only if you go all in.

Nobody is going to do it for you. You've already decided that if you don't make the change, you're going to regret it. You've already decided that you deserve better. You've done all the calculations and figured out how you are going to mitigate the risk involved.

Now you have to take a deep breath, whisper profanity to yourself, and grab the opportunity by the balls. Quit that job, sell that old business, start that new job, start that side hustle, file for that divorce, ask them to marry you, talk to that beautiful person at the gym, throw the excuses off a skyscraper and get to work!

Reprogram Your Mind

In the beginning, taking action might feel like running up a muddy mountain during a flash flood. If you are past your early years, then other people's opinions won't won't mean anything, no matter how close you think you are to them. In the beginning, I advise that you don't share your journey with your coworkers if you work in an environment of rampant unfulfillment.

I learned to keep my mouth shut and let them all complain to each other every minute of every day and learned the power of compassion.

I learned to mentally repeat my affirmations and visualize my ideal day instead of letting my mind be programmed by their words. I would slam espresso in the car while driving to work and scream to myself.

"I am going to find my passion!"

"I am going to live the life of my wildest dreams!"

"I can do anything I put my mind to!"

After work, when I got into the car and had to fight off drifting to sleep, I would tell myself, "I have unlimited creativity, drive, and motivation to reach my goal."

The excitement and belief from my affirmations would wash over me, squashing down all previous self-doubt and exhaustion, getting me ready for my after-work passion hunt.

If I felt defeated or unsure of myself, I would visualize myself writing all the advice they gave me on a piece of paper. I would throw the paper in a blender and scatter the remains like confetti on top of a mountain during a hurricane.

You may notice yourself in a similar work situation as me. If so, you must focus on programing your own mind or subconsciously succumb to whatever your closest colleagues believe.

Learn to Love Sacrifice

Once you get a small taste of passion, you will do anything it takes to feel that again. The discomfort of trying new things, spending money and being horrible in the beginning feels like torture.

The greatest reward of all is in store for those who learn to love the journey. When you reach a point of loving making sacrifices, internal resistance within you falls away and you enter a deep flow. This momentum has the power to propel you into a whole new life.

You will look back in 5 years and won't even recognize yourself or your life once this snowball of momentum hits. When you get rewarded for doing a certain behavior, you will do it again and again just like a dope sick lab rat.

When we opt for going to a meetup group after work instead of cracking open a beer and watching our favorite sitcom, we are rewiring our brains. When you meet someone who is also on a journey of finding what they love in life, all the struggle will feel immediately worth it. When you have a fellow knight on your crusade, you will feel like you can take on the whole world.

Sacrifices are temporary, lost time is permanent.

We may have to leave a toxic relationship.

We may have to give up spending our free time watching TV.

We may have to stop shopping.

We may have to minimize our time spent with unhappy friends who want to be victims instead of taking action.

You may have to find ways to get extra energy so you can work longer hours to find your passion such as exercise, eating healthy, and sleep. My favorite productivity hack is pursuing the habit of doing nothing during my work breaks.

You may even have to accept a job that gives you fewer hours and simplify your expenses to the best of your ability.

I know you may work 60-80 hours a week at your day jobs already, and the thought of adding more hours to find your passion seems infeasible. I too could have had a job working 60-80 hours a week. I turned down those offers and pursued a job that maxed out at 40 a week on purpose because I knew it would get me to my life goal quicker. If you have a family and responsibilities, then I totally understand why it is scary to accept a job for less money. I have mad love and respect for you. Do what you can in your free time even if it's only an hour a day in the morning before work. Your life of joy depends on it.

Did I get sick of eating brown rice, ground turkey and broccoli for breakfast, lunch, dinner and snacks? Yes, but the leverage I received from that time and money savings ended up paying me 100-fold down the road.

What balanced sacrifices can you make? This answer will vary from person to person, and I realize that your answer will be different. Find what works for YOU and your family. Ignore the rest.

Failure is Fun

I would rather fail 1 million times but be happy along the journey than be safe and feel "successful". Genuine success comes from taking action and failing continuously, as long as it's not the same failure twice. The first time we fail at something, we may never want to experience that feeling again. That teaches us to not reach too far next time.

They taught us in school that if we fail a test, then that is terrible and will ruin our future. The paradox is, the more we fail in the school of life, the happier and more fulfilled we will become when we learn from our mistakes.

I love failing now because I know that I am 1 step closer to accomplishing my goals. In the beginning, it was brutal on the ego. Working 40 hours a week on a business with a full-time job not only for free but to lose money is a brutal lesson that every entrepreneur will face in the beginning.

You learn quickly that you don't deserve anything just because you worked hard for it. The market speaks in dollars, and if my business was flawed, then I deserved the fate I got. I view these "failures" as another tuition bill from the school of life.

I would rather spend money chasing my dream than lose money analyzing my dream. Some amount of studying and learning is necessary in the beginning, but it turns into paralysis by analysis. Analyzing may give the insidious illusion of work when really, it's your brain seeking the easy way out.

Cash in on Your Passion

Do you see yourself putting money down on this interest or passion? When you put money down on your new identity, then it becomes real. When you have skin in the game, your hobby turns into a career. Invest money wisely into your passion and you will find a way to make it happen.

Taking the Scary Out of Change

From a young age, the way we learn is through fear. We learn to not touch the stove or we'll get burned. If we don't obey the law we go to jail, and if we get Fs in school, then we'll be a failure. The shootings, the virus, bombings, terrorists, and did I mention you're going to hell? Get realistic about your passion and obey the rules or you'll be a failure. I hope you are catching the irony. Even if these threats are for a good cause, these are all powerful mechanisms engineered to drive fear into the hearts of the masses to extract a desired result.

Powerful emotions = change.

We are programmed from many angles to respond to fear because emotions drive us to change.

But what if I told you that passion is more motivational than fear?

If you are unhappy and unfulfilled, then massive extreme action is the prescription. There are several tactics that make these extreme measures feel less painful in the short term and increase your threshold for pain in the long term. If we fail to execute these tactics properly, then we risk getting burned out. I go over how to increase your threshold for discomfort in my last book, *Ultimate Focus: The Art of Mastering Concentration*. Pushing yourself further than you thought you could go in incremental amounts will increase your threshold for pain. This goes for anything uncomfortable you do. Bonus points to those who do the exercises in the book.

Banish Perfectionism & Shame

Fear of failure is perfectionism. Perfectionism builds resistance, and resistance is the enemy of action. The clarity of who you are and what you love to do comes from action, not from resting on a bed of nails (for most of us).

Being shameful of acts we've done in the past or the commitments we haven't held is commonplace. We don't want to post anything online about our careers unless we are committed to executing our craft flawlessly over the next decade.

Well, I have news for you. All those people online who appear flawless? Remember how on average, 71% are miserable with their job according to that statistic from the Mental Health America and the FAAS?

The statistics say that you need not be worried for another minute, because comparing yourself to their social media self is a loser's bargain. Success is inevitable for the courageous. The cost of playing it safe is never truly living. There will always be someone that doesn't like something in this world. There are people who don't like to travel, don't like comedians, or don't even like coffee. I would not spend another minute being worried about someone out there not liking you or your work. Be authentic and let the world know what you are made of.

Show Imposter Syndrome Who's Boss

"Whether you think you can or can't, you are right." ~Henry Ford

Imposter syndrome is when you feel out of place among your desired colleagues. They all know you are qualified to be there, but you don't believe that you are one of them.

This could not be farther from the truth. Imposter syndrome is an insidious disguise for being realistic with yourself. If it is your first day on the job as an airline pilot or surgeon, then you should listen to that fear within reason.

I will bet that the consequence of being wrong is not life or death for most of us. If we believe we can do something, then our subconscious mind and conscious mind will work together synergistically to make it happen.

Most people are their own meanest critic. Renowned Psychotherapist Amy Morrison says in an Inc. article on self-criticism, "it's easier to be compassionate towards other people than yourself. You may call yourself an idiot, but it's unlikely that you'd say that to a loved one." She believes that we are more prone to seeing the bad in ourselves than we are in others.

Next time you get that sinking feeling of self-doubt in your stomach, try imagining the worst-case scenario of what would happen if you failed. Would anyone die? Would you have to be homeless? Most of the time, what we are afraid of is not as drastic as we thought. When you realize that the worst-case scenario is not that terrible, then it becomes easier to move on and not let your inner critic get in your way.

Lastly, be patient with yourself or I will find you. Most of us have spent years feeding our invasive inner critic a healthy diet. It will take time to make them shrivel up and die, but when they do, it will mean a life of freedom. You have earned all you have accomplished and you deserve the credit.

Be Polarizing

To find your passion, you must learn to surrender to yourself and authentically be yourself. Many of us are under the illusion that we are professionals in our career. The truth is, we are award-winning actors. We wake up, take a shower, throw on our costumes (suit and tie). Then act "professional" in front of our colleagues, clients or employees. We have one aspect of this funny equation correct. We are very good at faking it until we make it.

When we act in a way that those around us approve of, we get validation. Through positive reinforcement, our experiences mold our identities. Eventually we become who everyone around us wants us to be. We pretend to be someone we are not to impress people we might not even like or get validation from those we do like. Soon we are so contorted and disfigured that we don't resonate with whom we are anymore. We don't recognize ourselves but feel like we have to keep up the identity we built.

When we have found our passion, we can be our authentic self. Our authentic self operates from the heart. Everything we say, do, feel, and act, must come from our genuine heart space. Sometimes we have to look down at the clown costume we are wearing and tear it off.

To operate at our full capacity, we have to turn off our analytical mind and relax fully into the moment. To fully relax into the moment, we need to be our authentic self. The state of being completely immersed in the activity one is doing is popularly called the flow state. One of the easiest ways to hit the flow state is to be your authentic self.

There is a time and place to act and be a certain way. The same vulgar jokes that have your friends rolling back, crying tears of joy, are not as appreciated at Christmas dinner with your in-laws or in front of a prospective client.

There is a balance to this art. My only point is to monitor yourself and realize when you lose your authenticity. Being Polarizing will make people either love or hate you. That is scary and why many people avoid being their authentic self.

When you change your identity, the people in your life might not be too fond of it. Some may say, "you changed," with a negative connotation. If someone doesn't like the real you, then they just did you a favor by leaving your life. I'd rather have more haters and more lovers than only people indifferent about me. The people that stick around will truly love you for who you are and that feels better than any rejection.

Let the haters fall away, they weren't meant to be in your life. You will find that the people you have left in your life will love you more.

Sustain the Momentum

Finding and sustaining your passion is a process. You will constantly reiterate, test, prototype and perfect what works for you. You will learn to find joy in the pain of change. The pain will happen, but suffering during the journey is a choice. Choose to keep pressing onward. The more painful the experience, the more satisfying the reward. Similar to trekking up a mountain. Once you get to the top, the endorphins and stunning view will make the struggle and sometimes downright terrifying ascent worth it, leaving you craving more.

Summary

I am so proud of you for making it this far. More importantly, you should feel proud of yourself, because I guarantee you the masses gave up already. The fact that you read this book this far speaks volumes to what you will accomplish down the road. You have amazing things coming your way. A life of passion and joy is not deserved. It is earned and you have proven that you are capable of accomplishing anything you desire. Keep pushing on before I get all emotional.

Action Steps:

- Take a piece of paper and fold it in half hot dog style. Keep the paper and a pencil in your pocket and throughout the course of the day. Write down your thoughts in the left column. At the end of the week you will have a collection of thoughts, some helpful and others destructive.

- In the right-hand column write down your new belief that will replace this old damaging belief.

- Setup a monthly auto deposit to a savings account to put money aside for your new passion.
- When times get hard, you will need to refer back to your personal why. Write down exactly why you want to pursue this career on a personal level.

As an independent author, it can be challenging to get my voice heard. If you want to aid my mission of helping as many people as possible achieve freedom, then please consider leaving a brief, honest review.

Even just a few sentences would be tremendously helpful.

The more reviews my books get, the more people I will reach, the more lives I will help through my books, and the more I will have to donate to Hagar. Hagar is a human trafficking and slavery victim charity based out of Vietnam, Cambodia, Afghanistan and Singapore.

Feel free to reach out at chandler@chandlerkitching.com, I love reading fan mail! To the few of you that have left a review, I am forever in your debt. You are the reason I wake up at 5 am with my heart pounding and ready to write. From the bottom of my heart, thank you.

Visit this link or scan the QR code:

http://www.amazon.com/gp/customer-reviews/write-a-review.html?asin=B08LPHWVTL

Sincerely,

Chandler

Afterword

You're lying in bed; heart is pounding, and it's never felt so good to be alive. It's 5 am Monday morning, and every second you lay longer in bed is like a splinter growing in your mind, driving you mad.

You spring out of bed ready to tackle your favorite problems. You know that every minute you spend solving these problems, the world changes for the better. Looking forward to Monday is not only feasible, but also attainable through persistent and continuous action.

You may not stay in the same career your entire life and that is understandable. With the exponential growth of artificial intelligence, the job market is set to change drastically. Gartner, Inc., the world's leading research company, predicts that AI will produce more jobs than it removes. So, my point is to embrace this journey of transformation and change, our careers don't have to be the same our whole life.

Many sayings we are told warn us the perils of quitting such as, "the grass is always greener" or avoid "shiny object syndrome". This is true only in the aspect that sometimes we quit too early when challenges arise, especially if one works for themselves. However, we must remember my analogy of not marrying the first crush we had in middle school. If we truly stood the trials of time and rose above the challenges of the job and are still sick of the day in day out drudgery, then QUIT. Plan your escape strategically and execute fearlessly.

Amassing insane amounts of wealth is definitely possible while living a life you love. Usually we have to be willing to take the less secure route or work for less in the beginning to feel the long-term results. Working for passion is a long-term play. Working for solely money or power is a short-term play.

Be grateful for yobelur failures. I am so grateful and happy for these experiences, and I wouldn't trade them for anything in the world. They taught me the skills I needed to build my dream life later down the road.

Sometimes your situation may feel grim and hopeless. The key, I want you to understand is to never give up. Once you mentally give up on your dream life, then you are sentenced to a life of regret. Do whatever you have to do to find your passion because failure weighs ounces while regret weighs pounds.

I am excited beyond belief for you. Once you find your passion, your energy will skyrocket to additional levels, your relationships will deepen and your health will improve. When you find your passion, this new joy will spill over and affect every single area of your life.

No matter where you are in life, you always have the power to turn your life around. Jump into the driver's seat, turn off the AI hive mind auto driving car, slam on the brakes and take the U turn before it's too late.

The universe can alter lives in the blink of an eye. Living for another day is not a right, it's a privilege. You have a 1 in 700,000 chance of dying from an asteroid hitting you, according to astronomer Alan Harris. Do not waste another moment of this precious, wonderful life, pursue your passion and cherish every moment as if it's your last. Then and only then, will you live a life that most can only dream of.

When you are using your greatest strengths to solve your favorite problems, you operate at a whole new level of efficiency, desire and drive. You no longer measure your workweeks in hours, instead you measure in results.

If everyone in the world unlocked their full potential and woke up ecstatic to tackle global issues, then the world would blossom into a stunning garden of dreams actualized. It is our moral, ethical, obligation and duty to find our passion so we can give the best we have to offer to all humanity.

So next time you catch an adult asking a child "what do you *want* to be when they grow up?", step in and ask the kid, "what *problem* do you want to solve when you grow up?"

My Other Books You'll Love

Ultimate Focus:
The Art of Mastering Concentration

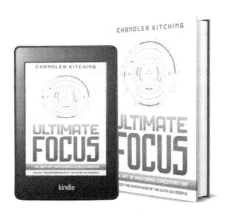

The Art of Doing Nothing:
The No-Guilt Practical Burnout Recovery System for Busy Professionals

References

Alumni, S. (2018, April 24). *How to (not) find your passion - Stanford Alumni*. Medium. https://medium.com/stanford-alumni/ho w-to-not-find-your-passion-d74f33f0296e

Careers Advice Online. (2020, June 27). *Career Change Statistics*. http://careers-advice-online.com/career-change-statistics.html#:%7E:text=The%20average %20person%20will%20change,or%20jobs %20every%2012%20months.

Drucker, R. D. (2020, October 10). *Edwin C. Barnes from Rags to Riches*. Bridge to Strength. https://www.bridgetostrength.com/article s/rags-to-riches/#:%7E:text=In %201951%2C%20nearly

%2046%20years,Barnes%20retired %20from%20business%20life.

Evan Carmichael. (2016, April 20). *How Stephen King Wrote Some of His BEST BOOKS! | Top 10 Rules* [Video]. YouTube. https://www.youtube.com/watch?v=f_Bh-yNpUpI&t=555s

Grant, A. G. (2014, August 1). *How Customers Can Rally Your Troops*. Harvard Business Review. https://hbr.org/2011/06/how-customers-can-rally-your-troops

Howard, B. C. H. (2016, February 9). *What Are the Odds a Meteorite Could Kill You?* National Geographic. https://www.nationalgeographic.com/news/2016/02/160209-meteorite-death-india-probability-odds/

Ignita Office. (2020, January 3). *A Harvard*

Study: The Science of Happiness.
https://www.ignitiaoffice.com/the-science-of-happiness-a-harvard-study/

Johnson, S. (2019, December 5). *The prefrontal cortex, cerebellum and reward systems.* Big Think. https://bigthink.com/mind-brain/adult-brain?
rebelltitem=2#rebelltitem2

Marks, G. M. (2017, October 19). *Study: 71 percent of employees are looking for new jobs.* Washington Post.
https://www.washingtonpost.com/gdpr-consent/?next_url=https%3a%2f
%2fwww.washingtonpost.com%2fnews
%2fon-small-business%2fwp
%2f2017%2f10%2f19%2fstudy-71-percent-of-employees-are-looking-for-new-jobs%2f

Mentor, M. M. (2020, September 20). *615 - 5*

Steps to Kick Imposter Syndrome to the Curb from Modern Mentor. Stitcher Modern Mentor Podcast. https://www.stitcher.com/podcast/moder n-mentor/e/77908610?autoplay=true

PCA Global. (2017, October 11). *The logical reasons to trust your gut feeling*. https://pca-global.com/logical-reasons-to-trust-your-gut-feeling/

Plait, P. (2019, November 5). *Death by meteorite*. Discover Magazine. https://www.discovermagazine.com/the-sciences/death-by-meteorite#.UR5QRx03uxo

Plumer, B. P. (2013, May 20). *Only 27 percent of college grads have a job related to their major*. Washington Post. https://www.washingtonpost.com/gdpr-

consent/?next_url=https%3a%2f
%2fwww.washingtonpost.com%2fnews
%2fwonk%2fwp
%2f2013%2f05%2f20%2fonly-27-percent-
of-college-grads-have-a-job-related-to-
their-major%2f

Shaw, K. S. (2017, February 22). *Travel broadens
the mind, but can it alter the brain?* The
Guardian.
https://www.theguardian.com/education/
2016/jan/18/travel-broadens-the-mind-
but-can-it-alter-the-brain

Steiner, S. S. (2013, December 6). *The 5 Things
People Regret Most On Their Deathbed.*
Business Insider.
https://www.businessinsider.com/5-
things-people-regret-on-their-deathbed-
2013-12?international=true&r=US&IR=T

TEDx. (2017, May 19). *Designing Your Life | Bill Burnett | TEDxStanford* [Video]. Youtube. https://www.youtube.com/watch?v=SemHh0n19LA

The 80, B. T. A. H. T. (2020, September 28). *Our new guide to doing good with your career*. 80,000 Hours. https://80000hours.org/key-ideas/

Wagorn, P. W. (2014, April 11). *Burn the Ships*. IdeaConnection. https://www.ideaconnection.com/blog/open+innovation/open-innovation-commitment.html

Wired Lab. (2018, April 4). *AI and the Future of Work*. AI and the Future of Work | WIRED. https://www.wired.com/wiredinsider/2018/04/ai-future-work/

Printed in Great Britain
by Amazon